Barrel of Monkeys Super Silly Joke Book

by
Dave Ross

illustrated by
Jared Chapman

STERLING

New York / London
www.sterlingpublishing.com/kids

D0168143

STERLING and the distinctive Sterling logo are
registered trademarks of Sterling Publishing Co., Inc.

Library of Congress Cataloging-in-Publication Data

Ross, Dave, 1949-
Barrel of monkeys : super silly joke book /
by Dave Ross ; illustrated by Jared Chapman.
p. cm.
ISBN 978-1-4027-5362-6
1. Monkeys—Juvenile humor. I. Title.
PN6231.M663R67 2008
818'.5402—dc22
2007041138

10 9 8 7 6 5 4 3 2 1

Published by Sterling Publishing Co., Inc.
387 Park Avenue South, New York, NY 10016
Text © 2008 by Hasbro
Illustrations © 2008 by Jared Chapman
Distributed in Canada by Sterling Publishing
C/o Canadian Manda Group, 165 Dufferin Street
Toronto, Ontario, Canada M6K 3H6
Distributed in the United Kingdom by GMC
Distribution Services Castle Place, 166 High Street,
Lewes, East Sussex, England BN7 1XU
Distributed in Australia by Capricorn Link (Australia)
Pty. Ltd. P.O. Box 704, Windsor, NSW 2756, Australia

Sterling ISBN-13: 978-1-4027-5362-6
          ISBN-10: 1-4027-5362-4

For information about custom editions, special sales,
premium and corporate purchases, please contact
Sterling Special Sales Department at 800-805-5489
or specialsales@sterlingpublishing.com.

table of contents

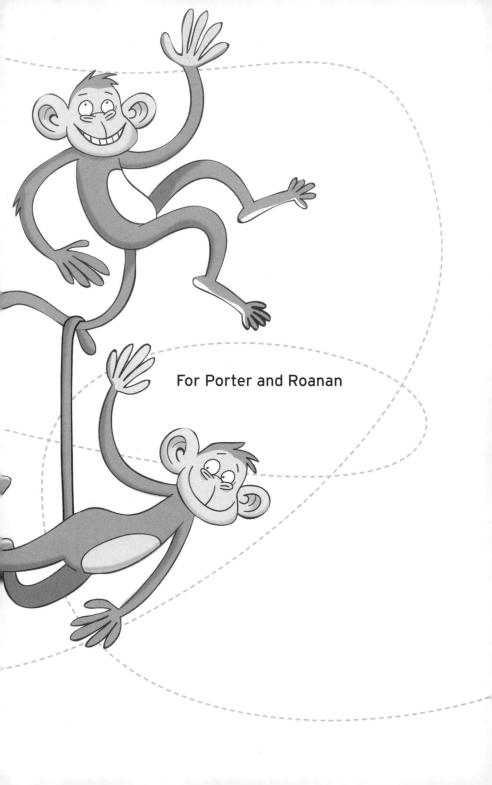

For Porter and Roanan

it's a jungle out there

Why don't monkeys play cards in the jungle?

Too many cheetahs.

Why is it dangerous to do math in the jungle?

If you add 4 and 4, you get 8.

What do jaguars call monkeys?

Delicious.

How do monkeys see jackals at night?

They use jackal lanterns.

What did the leopard say after eating the monkey?

"That really hit the spot."

What did the monkey say when the panther bit his tail?

"That's the end of me."

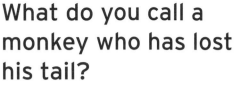

What do you call a monkey who has lost his tail?

Detailed.

Why didn't the monkey spot the leopard?

He didn't have to; leopards are born with spots.

Why didn't the monkey believe the tiger?

He thought he was a lion.

What did the crocodile say to the monkey?

"Pleased to eat you."

Do rain forest monkeys use a bathtub?

No, but they take lots of showers.

Did you hear about the monkey that caught an electric eel?

He was shocked.

Did you hear about the monkey who wouldn't share his clams?

He was shellfish.

don't feed the monkey

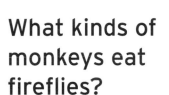

What kinds of monkeys eat fireflies?

Those that want a light snack.

What kinds of monkeys eat roadrunners?

Those who like fast food.

What kinds of monkeys eat snails?

Those who don't like fast food.

What did the chimp say to the termite?

"Wood you like to join me for dinner?"

Why did the monkey bite the tightrope walker?

He wanted a balanced diet.

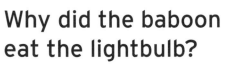

Why did the baboon eat the lightbulb?

He thought it was a bright idea.

Did you hear about
the monkey who ate a
canary on Halloween?
He thought it was trick or tweet.

Did you hear about the
new hybrid monkey?
Runs on either peanuts or bananas.

What has hairy
knuckles, six legs,
and eats bananas?
Three monkeys.

Why don't
monkeys eat
frogs?
It makes them croak.

How do you make a baboon stew?

Make him wait three hours for dinner.

Where do monkeys barbeque?

On grillas.

What happened after the monkey swallowed the spoon?

Nothing. He was unable to stir.

12

Do gibbons eat birds?

Only if they're in a fowl mood.

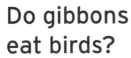

What do you call an overweight baboon?

A chunky-monkey.

What did the banana say to the monkey?

"Want to grab a bite?"

Is monkey soup good for your health?
Not if you're the monkey.

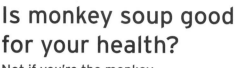

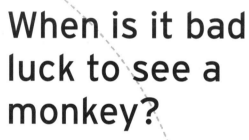

When is it bad luck to see a monkey?
When you're a banana.

Did you hear about the monkeys who looked for bananas in a coconut tree?
It was a fruitless search.
(It was a nutty idea, too.)

monkey favorites

What's a monkey's favorite month?

Ape-ril.

What's a monkey's favorite dance?

The Orangutango.

What's a monkey's favorite flower?

Chimp-pansies.

What's a monkey's favorite dessert?
Chocolate chimp cookies.

What's a monkey's favorite toy?
A boom-orang.

What's a monkey's favorite Christmas carol?
"Jungle Bells."

What did the monkey top his lemon pie with?

Meranguetan!

What should you do if your baboon gets loose?

Tighten him with a monkey wrench.

What's black and white and has sixteen wheels?

A capuchin wearing roller skates!

What do you call a hurricane named for an ape?

Typhoon Baboon.

What do you call a chimp without an eye?

Chmp.

What do you call a chimp with three eyes?

Chiiimp.

What do you call a gullible monkey?

A chump.

How many baboons does it take to change a lightbulb?

We don't know. So far, all they do is break the ladder.

monkey nonsense

Why did the monkey pull the plug on his refrigerator?

He wanted to see it lose its cool.

Which kind of monkey can jump higher than a house?

All of them; houses can't jump.

What do you find inside baboons?

Ba-bones.

Why aren't monkey noses 12 inches long?

Because then they would be a foot.

How do monkeys get down the stairs?

They slide down the banana-ster.

What do you call a monkey at the North Pole?

Lost!

When is a monkey like a rock?

When he's a little bolder.

What did the monkey say to the toilet?

"You look a bit flushed."

Why don't you ever see an ad for a lost monkey in the newspaper?

Because monkeys don't read newspapers.

What time did the monkey go to the dentist?

Tooth-hurty.

What's smarter than a talking monkey?

A spelling bee.

Where do itchy monkeys shop?

The flea market.

Why won't monkeys pay $10 apiece for bananas?

Because they want whole ones.

Why do monkeys scratch themselves?

Nobody else knows where they itch.

What's so difficult about writing a report on monkeys?

It's easier to write the report on paper.

Why shouldn't you gossip in front of monkeys?

They all carry tails.

Why did the monkey ride the pony?

He was horsing around.

If a monkey lost his tail what would he do?

Go to any retail store.

Which monkeys have long tails?

The ones who don't like short stories.

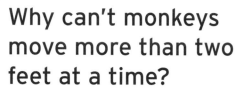

Why can't monkeys move more than two feet at a time?

They were only born with two feet.

What kind of monkeys talk too much?

Blab-boons.

How does a monkey say "I'm sorry"?

He offers an ape-ology.

What kinds of monkeys live in rain forests?

Wet ones.

What is beautiful, hairy, and wears glass slippers?

Cindorilla.

Who helped Cindorilla get to the ball?

Her hairy godmother.

What would you get if you threw a brown monkey in the Black Sea?

A wet monkey.

What would you get if you threw a gorilla in the White Sea?

Black and blue. Gorillas don't like to swim.

What would you get if you threw a plaid monkey in the Red Sea?

Nothing. There are no plaid monkeys.

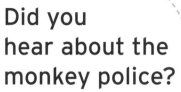

Did you hear about the monkey police?

They enforce the law of the jungle.

What's black on the outside, furry inside, and travels underwater?

A submarine full of monkeys.

Why are most monkeys uninterested in politics?

Because they are ape-olitical.

monkey tales

What to Do If You Find a Monkey

A man was walking down the street and found a monkey. He took the monkey by the hand and went to find a policeman.

The policeman said, "Take the monkey to the zoo."

The next day the policeman saw the same man walking down the street with the monkey. He said, "I thought I told you to take the monkey to the zoo!"

The man replied, "I did. We had so much fun that today we are going to the movies."

Does Your Monkey Bite?

A man sees a young boy and a monkey sitting on a park bench. The monkey looks very cute. The man asks, "Does your monkey bite?"

The little boy says, "No."

So the man reaches out to pat the monkey on the head and, chomp. The monkey bites the man's hand.

"Ouch!" shouts the man. "I thought you said your monkey doesn't bite."

The boy smiles and says, "It's not my monkey."

Not a Bright Idea

Did you hear about the monkey who swallowed a lamp and went to a veterinarian to have it removed?

No, what happened?

The monkey was delighted.

Monkey Marriage

Did you hear about the monkey who married the kangaroo?

The relationship had its ups and downs, but eventually they lived hoppily ever after.

Monkey Sundae

A monkey walks into a drugstore and orders a one-dollar sundae. He puts down a ten-dollar bill to pay for it.

The clerk thinks, "What can a monkey know about money?" So he hands back a single dollar in change and says, "You know, we don't get many monkeys in here."

"No wonder," answers the monkey. "At these prices you won't get many more."

easy-to-follow directions

**What should you do
with a blue monkey?**

Cheer him up.

**What do you do with
a green monkey?**

Wait until he ripens.

**What should you do
with a red monkey?**

Stop embarrassing him.

**Why did the monkey
buy twelve canaries?**

He heard they were cheeper by the dozen.

**How do you stop a
baboon from charging?**

Unplug him.

When is a monkey most like a bicycle?

When he's too tired.

What do you call a small bed for a chimp?

An apricot.

What do award-winning monkeys receive?

A blue gibbon.

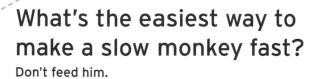

What's the easiest way to make a slow monkey fast?

Don't feed him.

monkeys on vacation

Where do monkeys vacation?
"Someplace that swings."

Where do monkeys go for a boat ride?
The baboondocks.

When do monkeys go on vacation?
Sometime during Ape-ril.

Why did the monkey jump in the ocean?

He wanted wavy hair.

What did the monkey say to the ocean?

"Shore am glad to sea you."

How did the monkey say goodbye to the beach?

He just waved.

Why did the monkey cross the sea?

To get to the other tide.

How do you quiet a sea monkey?

Tell him to clam up.

a monkey by any other name

Where could you find a handy monkey?

In a palm tree.

What would you call a wise guy monkey?

A chimpunk.

What do you call a monkey hissy fit?

An orangu-tantrum.

What do you call a monkey mess-up?

A baboon-doggle.

What do you call a monkey that keeps coming back?

A baboomerang.

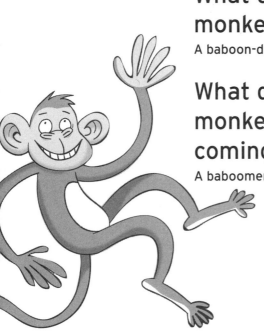

What do you call a woolly monkey who picks on smaller monkeys?

A woolly bully.

Why is a monkey's nose in the middle of his face?

Because it's the scenter.

Why can't you take a picture of a marmoset with a banana?

Bananas can't take pictures, you need a camera.

What do you call a lazy monkey?

A couch banana.

How do you catch a squirrel monkey?

Climb a tree and act like a nut.

If baboons boogie and orangutans tango, what do tree monkeys do?

Swing dance.

Did you hear about the baby ape?

He was a chimp off the old block.

Do monkeys sunburn?

No, but orangu-tans.

Did you hear about the monkey who was scared of lions?

He had clawstrophobia.

What did the monkey say to his niece?

"I'll be a monkey's uncle."

why did the monkey cross the road?

Why did the chimpanzee cross the road?

To take care of some monkey business.

Why did the baboon cross the road?

To prove he wasn't chicken.

Why did the monkey cross the road with a chicken?

For some fowl reason.

Why did the monkey take the cow across the street?

To get to the udder side.

Why did the gorilla cross the road?

Because he wanted to. You got a problem with that?

Why did the monkey cross the jungle?

To get to the other vine.

Why did the monkey cross the playground?

To get to the other slide.

barrel of monkey business

Is a barrel full of monkeys fun?

Ape-solutely!

What would you call a barrel of gorillas?

A ton of fun.

What's more fun than a barrel of monkeys?

Two barrels of monkeys.

Where would you find a barrel of monkeys?

I don't know, it depends on where they were lost.

What do you call 12 orangutans in a barrel?

An orangu-tangle.

Why was the monkey kicked out of the barrel?

He got fired for too much monkey business.

Where could you find a barrel full of spider monkeys?

On the Web, of course.

gorilla my dreams

What's the best way to call a gorilla?

Long distance!

What is white, cold and hairy, and breaks ice cream cones?

A scoop of vanilla gorilla.

What do you get when you cross a gorilla with a parakeet?

I don't know, but when it talks you'd better listen.

What do you call a 1,000 pound gorilla?

Sir.

What should you do if you're in the jungle by yourself and a gorilla charges you?

Pay him.

What is the best thing to do if you find a gorilla in your bed?

Sleep somewhere else.

Why do gorillas have such big nostrils?

Because they have big fingers.

Why don't kangaroos like gorillas?

They make them feel jumpy.

What happens when a gorilla rips the muffler off a car?

He gets exhausted.

What time is it when a gorilla rides your bicycle?

Time to get a new bicycle!

Did you hear about the gorilla that tried to get into a barrel?

He could hardly contain himself.

What's green and weighs 400 pounds?

A seasick gorilla.

What should you give a seasick gorilla?

Plenty of room.

What did the grape say when the gorilla stepped on it?

Nothing. It just let out a little wine.

How do you get down off a gorilla?

You don't. You get down off a goose.

king kong sized monkey business

Why did King
Kong climb the
Empire State
Building?
He needed to catch a plane.

Why did King Kong climb the Empire State Building?
Because he couldn't fit in the elevator!

Why did King Kong climb the library?
The building had thousands of stories.

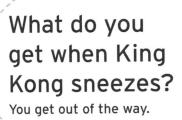

What do you get when King Kong sneezes?

You get out of the way.

Why did the cop give King Kong a ticket?

He ran a stomp sign.

How do you take King Kong for a walk?

First, get a really big leash.

What happened when King Kong ran away with the circus?

The police made him give it back.

What's King Kong's favorite food?

Squash.

What is as big as King Kong but doesn't weigh anything?

King Kong's shadow.

What do you say to King Kong when he's angry?

Nothing. You run.

What should you do if you find King Kong sitting in your chair?

Find somewhere else to sit.

How many bananas can King Kong eat?

As many as he wants.

going bananas

What did the monkey say to the banana?
"It's been nice gnawing you."

What is the easiest way to make a banana split?
Cut it in half.

What did the banana say to the monkey?
Nothing. Bananas don't talk!

If twenty monkeys run after one banana, what time is it?
Twenty after one!

Why are bananas never lonely?

Because they hang around in bunches.

A seven-year-old baboon named Bruce works in the banana store. He sells bananas for 7 cents a pound. He gets up at seven in the morning and goes to bed at seven every night. What does Bruce weigh?

Bananas.

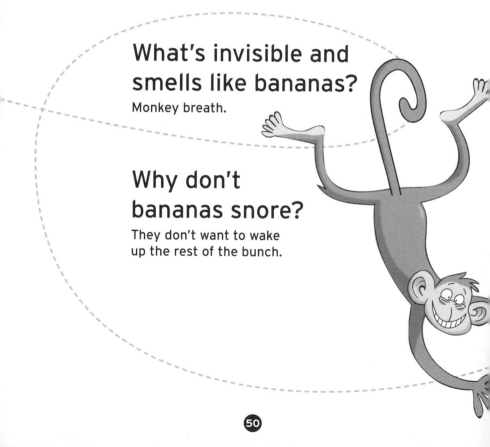

What's invisible and smells like bananas?

Monkey breath.

Why don't bananas snore?

They don't want to wake up the rest of the bunch.

Are bananas good for your eyes?

Sure, you ever see a monkey wearing glasses?

What's brown and yellow, brown and yellow, brown and yellow?

A monkey rolling down a hill with a banana.

What do monkeys call bananas?

Dinner.

Why did the banana go to the doctor?

He wasn't peeling well.

What do bananas say when they answer the phone?
"Yellow!"

Why was the sunburned banana embarrassed?
She was starting to peel.

A banana and an orange were on a high diving board. The orange jumped off. Why didn't the banana?
Because it was yellow.

Why did banana #2 quit the bunch?
He was tired of playing second banana.

What happens when you throw one banana to two monkeys?

Banana split.

Did you hear about the banana stopwatch?

It had split-second timing.

What do you call two banana peels?

A pair of slippers!

What do gorillas call a bunch of bananas?

Ape-etizers.

Did you hear about the farmer who got rich with his banana crop?

He made a bunch.

What do you call a rude banana?

Fresh fruit.

How many bananas does it take to screw in a lightbulb?

A bunch!

What would you get if you crossed a bee with a banana?

A honey-bunch.

In what sport do bananas compete?

Track and peeled.

What's the first thing an orangutan learns in school?
The ape b c's!

Have they proved the Abominable Snowman is an ape?

Not yeti.

What sound does an exploding monkey make?
BA-BOOM!

What happened to the ape that ate his keys?
He got lockjaw.

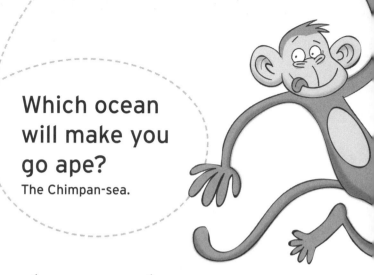

Which ocean will make you go ape?

The Chimpan-sea.

How do monkeys get clean?

They wait for Ape-ril showers.

Is there a monkey in Massachusetts?

No, but there's an ape in Cape Cod.

Where do monkeys hear rumors?

Through the apevine.

Did you hear about the flying monkey?

He was a hot air baboon.

there's a monkey at the door

Knock-knock.
Who's there?
Beryl.
Beryl who?
Beryl of monkeys.

Knock-knock.
Who's there?
Lettuce.
Lettuce who?
**Lettuce play
Barrel of Monkeys.**

Knock-knock.
Who's there?
Justin.
Justin who?
**Justin time
for another
monkey joke.**

Knock-knock.
Who's there?
Anita.
Anita who?
**Anita 'nother
monkey joke.**

Knock-knock.
Who's there?
Juneau.
Juneau who?
Juneau any jungle jokes?

Knock-knock.
Who's there?
Gorilla.
Gorilla who?
Gorilla cheese sandwich for me, please.

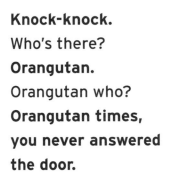

Knock-knock.
Who's there?
Orangutan.
Orangutan who?
Orangutan times, you never answered the door.

Knock-knock.
Who's there?
Lemur.
Lemur who?
Lemur know if you've had enough knock-knocks.

Knock-knock.
Who's there?
Monkey
Monkey who?
**Monkey see,
monkey do!**

Knock-knock.
Who's there?
Dishes.
Dishes who?
**Dishes da monkey,
gimme a banana.**

Knock-knock.
Who's there?
Fred.
Fred who?
**Fred any good
monkey jokes lately?**

Knock-knock.
Who's there?
Handsome.
Handsome who?
**Handsome bananas
to the monkey.**

Knock-knock.
Who's there?
Howie.
Howie who?
**Howie doin' with
the monkey jokes?**

Knock-knock.
Who's there?
Safari.
Safari who?
Safari, so good.

Knock-knock.
Who's there?
Dishwasher.
Dishwasher who?
**Dishwasher last
knock-knock joke.**

oldies but goodies

Where was the
monkey when the
lights went out?

In the dark.

What's the difference
between monkeys and
peanut butter?

If you don't know, I don't want you
making my sandwich.

How can you tell if
there are 100 monkeys
in your refrigerator?

The door won't shut.

What's the difference between a monkey and a flea?

A monkey can have fleas, but a flea cannot have monkeys.

What is a baby monkey after it is four days old?

Five days old.

Which side of a monkey has more hair?

The outside.

What three keys will not open a door?

Turkeys, donkeys, and monkeys.

why you never see animals eating in a restaurant

A bunch of animals are eating at an expensive restaurant. When the waiter brings the check there is a problem.

The mallard says, "I'll have to duck this one."

The skunk says, "I only have one scent, and it's a bad one."

The crab says, "I'm a little pinched for cash."

The leopard says, "I'll pay if you spot me the doe."

The doe says, "I haven't got a buck with me."

The kangaroo says, "My pocket's empty."

The flamingo says, "Don't look at me, my bill's too big already."

The frog says, "I only have one greenback."

The turtle says, "I don't want to shell out for this."

The beaver says, "Ask the otters, I'll be dammed if I pay."

The snake says, "It's hiss turn."

The canary says, "I'm too cheep."

The bee says, "Buzz off."

The lion says, "Sorry. I've got no pride."

The monkey says, "As long as you'll take payment in bananas—I've got a bunch."

monkeys of the world

What do American monkeys eat?
Star-spangled bananas.

How can you tell if a monkey is Canadian?
He only climbs maple trees.

How can you tell if a monkey is from Iceland?

He is trying to defrost his banana.

Do Irish monkeys eat bananas?

Only the green ones.

How can you tell if a monkey is Russian?

He is moving very fast.

tarzan ticklers

How can you tell if Tarzan is in a bad mood?

He has a chimp on his shoulder.

Where does Tarzan work out?

At the jungle gym.

What does Tarzan call a show full of lions?

The mane event.

What does Tarzan call Jane?

His prime mate.

What do you get when you cross a lying ape with a long strip of cloth?

A fibbin' gibbon ribbon.

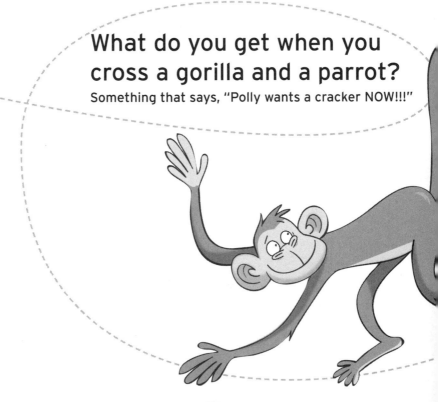

What do you get when you cross a gorilla and a parrot?

Something that says, "Polly wants a cracker NOW!!!"

What do you get when you cross a gorilla with a sparrow?

Broken telephone wires.

What do you get when you cross a sheep with a monkey?

A baaaa-boon.

What do you get when you cross a gorilla and a pigeon?

A real problem cleaning up after them.

What do you get when you combine a doorbell with a table tennis playing gorilla?

A King Kong Ping-Pong ding dong.

What do you get if you cross King Kong with a giant frog?

A hairy green monster that climbs up the Empire State Building and catches airplanes with its tongue.

What do you get when you cross King Kong with a kangaroo?

A trail of really big holes across Australia.

primate puzzlers

How Many Bananas?

Mr. and Mrs. Monkey found two bunches of really big bananas. Unfortunately, they were very far from home. They each picked up one bunch and started for home. They had only walked a short distance when Mr. Monkey began to complain that his load was too heavy. Mrs. Monkey turned to her husband and said, "I don't know what you're complaining about, because if you gave me one of your bananas, I would have twice as many as you, and if I gave you just one of mine, we would have equal loads." How many bananas were in each bunch the monkeys were carrying?

Answer: Mrs. Monkey's bunch had seven bananas and Mr. Monkey had five in his bunch.

How Many Monkeys?

Mr. and Mrs. Monkey have six daughters and each daughter has one brother. How many monkeys are in the Monkey family?

2 Many Monkeys

There are 2 monkeys in front of 2 other monkeys. There are 2 monkeys behind 2 other monkeys. There are 2 monkeys beside 2 other monkeys. How many monkeys are there?

Answer: 4

Answer: There are nine Monkeys in the family. Since each daughter shares the same brother, there are six girl monkeys, one boy monkey and Mr. and Mrs. Monkey.

The 5-Day Banana Gathering Contest

The monkeys decided to have a banana-gathering contest. The winner would be the monkey who gathered the most bananas after 5 days.

The winning monkey was gone for all 5 days and ended up with 30 bananas.

Each day, he gathered three more bananas than the day before.

How many bananas did the winning monkey gather on the first day?

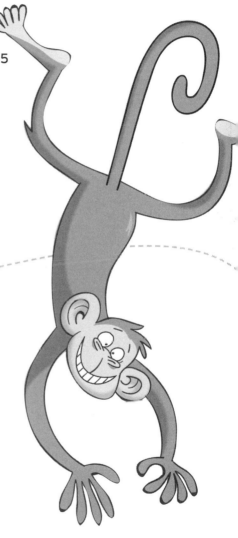

Answer: None. He didn't gather any bananas the first day, but he gathered 3 on the second day, 6 on the third day, 9 on the fourth day, and 12 on the fifth day.

The Mother Monkey Fruit Puzzle

Two mother monkeys and their two daughters were looking for fruit. They managed to find one banana, one orange, and one mango. Since only three pieces of fruit were found, how is it possible that they each took home a fruit?

Answer: The fruit-hunting party consisted of three monkeys. A grandmother monkey, a mother monkey, and a daughter. The mother monkey is both a mother and a daughter.

How Many Monkey Children?

There is a monkey family with both girl and boy monkeys. Each of the boy monkeys has the same number of brothers as he has sisters. Each of the girl monkeys has twice as many brothers as she has sisters. How many boys and girl monkeys are there in this family?

Why don't monkeys go out when it's raining cats and dogs?
They don't want to step in a poodle.

When is a monkey like a pony?
When he's a little hoarse.

Do monkeys go the library?

They visit some of the branches.

Why did the monkey move in with the horse?

It was a stable environment.

How do you get rid of an orangutan?

Perform an ape-endectomy.

Why did the scared monkey turn to stone?

He was petrified.

What happens when a monkey cracks up?

Rhesus pieces.

Why don't colobus monkeys hitchhike?

They do not have thumbs.

There were two monkeys hanging out in a tree. The first monkey said, "Ooo, ooo, ooo." The second monkey said, "Moo, moo, moo." The first monkey asked the second monkey, "Why did you say moo?" The second monkey said, "I'm learning a foreign language."

monkeys at the zoo

Did you hear about the amazing magic monkey on a moped?

He was driving down the street and turned into a zoo!

Why did the monkey bring a book to the zoo?

He wanted to read between the lions.

What did the monkey say to the wildebeests?

"Now I've herd everything."

Why did the monkey
stop arguing with the
porcupine?

He got the point.

Why couldn't
the monkey
call the zoo?

The lion was busy.

What did
the monkey
reporter
report?

All the bad gnus.

Why did the
monkey yawn
at the wild pig?

The pig was a boar.

How did the
monkey visit
the crocodile?

He took the allivator.

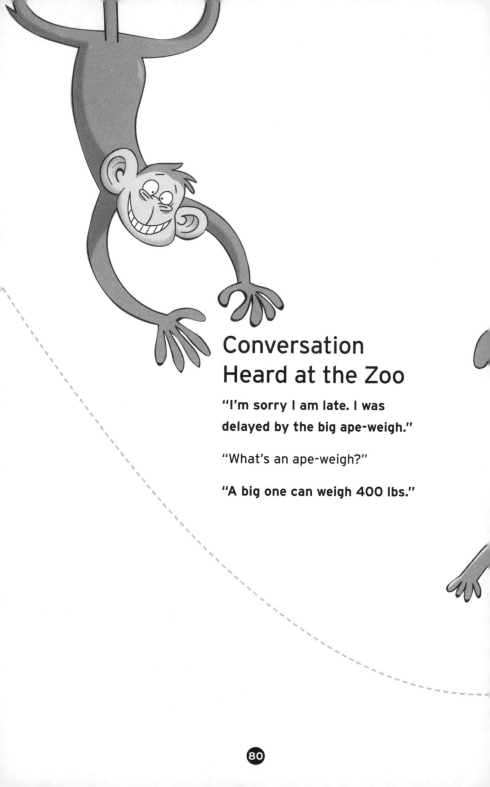

Conversation Heard at the Zoo

"I'm sorry I am late. I was delayed by the big ape-weigh."

"What's an ape-weigh?"

"A big one can weigh 400 lbs."

monkey see, monkey do

Can a monkey drive
a locomotive?

If you train him.

Can you train a monkey
to make bread?

Only if he kneads dough.

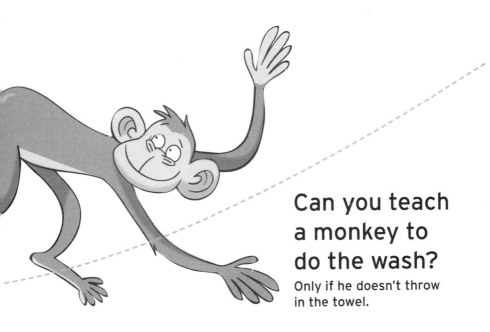

Can you teach
a monkey to
do the wash?

Only if he doesn't throw
in the towel.

Can you train a monkey to be a barber?

If you teach him all the shortcuts.

Can you train a monkey to be a doctor?

Only if he has enough patients.

Can you teach a monkey how to fish?

Once you get him hooked.

Is it easy to train monkeys to iron clothes?

No, they have to be pressed.

Why did the
monkey get
kicked out of
the orchestra?

He didn't know how to
conduct himself.

Can you
teach a
monkey
to be a
mountain
climber?

If he's so inclined.

Why was the monkey kicked out of chorus?

Because he got in treble!

Why did the monkey get fired from the deli?

He was full of baloney.

Can a monkey learn how to be a banker?

Not if he loses interest.

a rhesus rhyme and assorted ape poetry

There was a young rhesus from France,
whose hobby was searching for ants.
He took quite a spill,
on a tiny red hill,
and got up with ants in his pants.

A cheerful old ape at the zoo,
could always find something to do.
When it bored him, you know,
to walk to and fro,
he reversed it, and walked fro and to.

There was a young monkey
named Shepherd,
who was eaten for lunch by a leopard.
Said the leopard, "Egad!
You'd be tastier, lad,
if you had been salted and peppered!"

Said the crocodile to the ape from Bangkok,
"Would you like a lift from the dock?"
After the ride,
the ape was inside,
and a smile was on the face of the croc.

monkey say, monkey do

1. Say MONKEY before each word below:

Monkeys

About

Babbling

Baboon

Big

This

Got

I

Long

How

Look

2. Now say MONKEY
after each word:

Monkeys
About
Babbling
Baboon
Big
This
Got
I
Long
How
Look

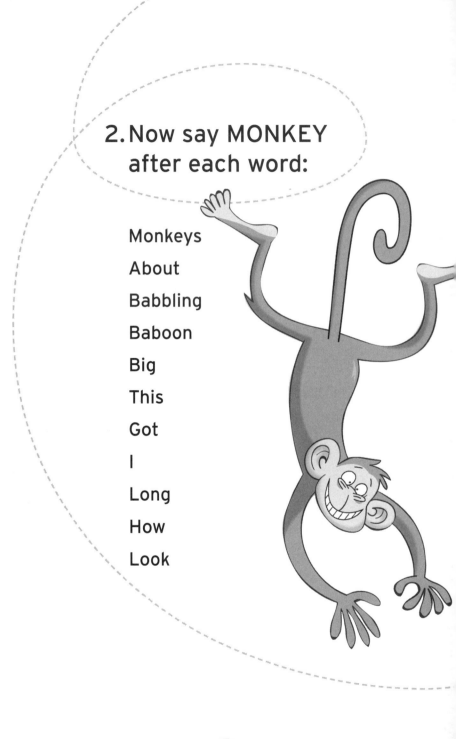

3. Start at the bottom and read the words upwards.

Monkeys

About

Babbling

Baboon

Big

This

Got

I

Long

How

Look

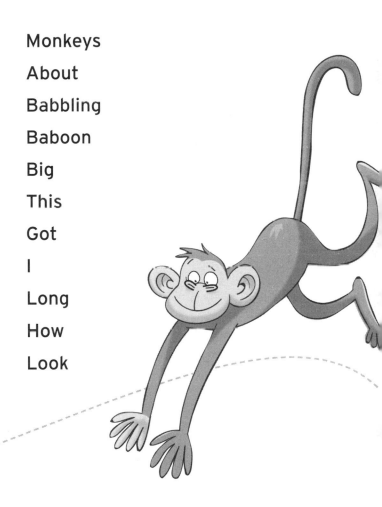

how to use monkey words

"More fun than a barrel of monkeys" is an idiom, or saying, that has been popular for over a hundred years. It is a way of expressing the humor of a person, place, or thing.

Correct usage: "This book is more fun than a barrel of monkeys."
Incorrect usage: "My sister looks like she crawled out of a barrel of monkeys."
Please note: While the second statement might be accurate, it would likely result in making your sister mad.

"I'll be a monkey's uncle!" This idiom is usually used to express surprise at something.

Correct usage: "When my brother told me he won the spelling bee, I said, 'I'll be a monkey's uncle!'"

Incorrect usage: "If my mom's sisters married baboons, they would be my monkey uncles."

"Monkey" or "monkeying" means to be mischievous, fool, trifle, or tamper with something.

Correct usage: "Stop monkeying with that computer and come play."

Incorrect usage: Although Walter wanted to monkey with the computer, it would not fit through the bars of Jo-Jo's cage.

Please note: Mashing bananas into the keyboard may be considered going beyond "monkeying" with a computer.

"Monkeyshines" is an old expression, more common about a hundred years ago. It was used to describe the simple pranks, or fooling around, of young children. These days, you only hear this word in really old, black-and-white movies...or from a grandparent.

Correct usage: "You children quit those monkeyshines and behave!"
Incorrect usage: "Lawrence, I do believe your monkey is quite thoroughly polished; you may discontinue your monkeyshines."

"Monkey bars" are a framework of metal pipes or bars for climbing. For many years, this type of equipment could be found on playgrounds.

Correct usage: "Hey, Dad. Look at me. I'm swinging from the monkey bars."
Incorrect usage: "Lloyd was disappointed when he realized monkey bars are not a new kind of candy bar."

"Make a monkey out of me" means to make a person look like a fool, or look foolish.
Correct usage: "You've made a monkey out of me for the last time, Marge."
Incorrect usage: "Marge, you've really made a monkey out of me; please give me a banana."

"Monkey business"
simply means silly
behavior.

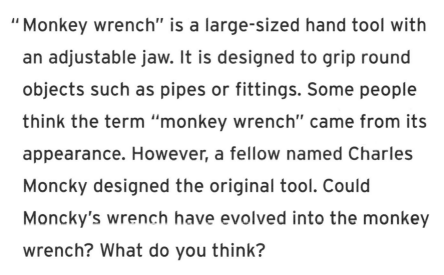

Correct usage: "What kind of
monkey business have you kids
been up to?"
Incorrect usage: "Ralph sold lots of baboons from
his monkey business."

"Monkey wrench" is a large-sized hand tool with
an adjustable jaw. It is designed to grip round
objects such as pipes or fittings. Some people
think the term "monkey wrench" came from its
appearance. However, a fellow named Charles
Moncky designed the original tool. Could
Moncky's wrench have evolved into the monkey
wrench? What do you think?

Correct usage: "Hey Louie, put the monkey wrench on that pipe
and tighten it up."
Incorrect usage: "Hey Charlie, my baboon is getting loose; tighten
it up with that monkey wrench."

Index